This journal belongs to

_____

Date

Priceless in value,
you are handcrafted by God,
who has a personal design
and plan for each of us.

You are a beloved child of God, precious to Him in every way.
As you seek Him, He will show you the mysteries of life
and unfold His unique plans for you—a life full of rich blessing
and peaceful assurance, using the gifts and experiences
that have made up who He has created you to be.

God cares about you and knows all the desires of your heart.
He is as close as breathing. Let this journal inspire you to express your thoughts,
record your prayers, embrace your dreams, and listen to what
God is saying to you about His blueprint with your name.

Be strong in the Lord, and may your soul find hope
in knowing that you are here by loving design.

*A*llow your dreams a place in your prayers and plans.
God-given dreams can help you move into the future He is preparing for you.

The LORD will work out his plans for my life—
for your faithful love, O LORD, endures forever.

PSALM 138:8 NLT

*D*reams carried around in one's heart for years, if they are dreams
that have God's approval, have a way of suddenly materializing.

CATHERINE MARSHALL

Delight yourself in the LORD; and He will give you the desires of your heart.

PSALM 37:4 NASB

The challenge of life is to take a single strand of a dream
and from it weave a beautiful reality.

Everything is possible to the one who believes.

MARK 9:23 HCSB

Imagination is the beginning of creation. You imagine what you desire, you will what you imagine, and at last you create what you will.

GEORGE BERNARD SHAW

May he give us the desire to do his will in everything.

1 KINGS 8:58 TLB

Nurture your mind with great thoughts; to believe in the heroic makes heroes.

BENJAMIN DISRAELI

O Lord, how great are Your works! Your thoughts are very deep.

*T*rust the past to the mercy of God, the present to His love,
and the future to His Providence.

AUGUSTINE

Let me experience Your faithful love in the morning, for I trust in You.
Reveal to me the way I should go because I long for You.

PSALM 143:8 HCSB

The moment you begin to delight in beauty, your heart and mind are raised.

BASIL HUME

*C*all to Me, and I will answer you, and show you
great and mighty things, which you do not know.

JEREMIAH 33:3 NKJV

Great faith isn't the ability to believe long and far into the misty future. It's simply taking God at His word and taking the next step.

What is faith? It is the confident assurance that something we want
is going to happen. It is the certainty that what we hope for is waiting for us,
even though we cannot see it up ahead.

HEBREWS 11:1 TLB

To appreciate beauty; to find the best in others; to give one's self;
to leave the world a little better...to know even one life has breathed easier
because you have lived.... This is to have succeeded.

RALPH WALDO EMERSON

Give, and it will be given to you. A good measure, pressed down,
shaken together and running over, will be poured into your lap.

LUKE 6:38 NIV

Look deep within yourself and recognize what brings life and grace into your heart. It is this that can be shared with those around you. You are loved by God. This is an inspiration to love.

CHRISTOPHER DE VINCK

God has given each of you some special abilities; be sure to use them to help each other, passing on to others God's many kinds of blessings.

1 Peter 4:10 TLB

We must not, in trying to think about how we can make a big difference, ignore the small, daily differences we can make, which, over time, add up to big differences that we often cannot foresee.

MARIAN WRIGHT EDELMAN

Serve one another humbly in love.

GALATIANS 5:13 NIV

The secret of life is that all we have and are is a gift of grace to be shared.

LLOYD JOHN OGILVIE

God has actually given us his Spirit (not the world's spirit) to tell us about the wonderful free gifts of grace and blessing that God has given us.

1 CORINTHIANS 2:12 TLB

Encouragement is awesome. It has the capacity to...actually change the course of another human being's day, week, or life.

CHARLES R. SWINDOLL

But encourage one another daily, as long as it is called "Today."

HEBREWS 3:13 NIV

If you're looking at 30 and you're scared, you still got it. If you're looking at 40 and you're scared, you still got it.... If you're 50, 60, 70, 80, God still has something for you.... Something you are uniquely called and equipped to do.

LIZ CURTIS HIGGS

*F*or the vision is yet for an appointed time.... Though it tarries, wait for it.

HABAKKUK 2:3 NKJV

*R*emember you are very special to God as His precious child.
He has promised to complete the good work He has begun in you.
As you continue to grow in Him, He will make you a blessing to others.

GARY SMALLEY AND JOHN TRENT

*H*e who began a good work in you will carry it on to completion
until the day of Christ Jesus.

PHILIPPIANS 1:6 NIV

We were not sent into this world to do anything into which we cannot put our hearts.

Whatever you do, do it enthusiastically, as something done for the Lord and not for men.

COLOSSIANS 3:23 HCSB

*U*se what talents you possess: the woods would be very silent
if no birds sang there except those that sang best.

HENRY VAN DYKE

It is God who is at work in you, both to will
and to work for His good pleasure.

PHILIPPIANS 2:13 NASB

The patterns of our days are always rearranging...and each design for living is unique, graced with its own special beauty.

All the days ordained for me were written in your book before one of them came to be.

PSALM 139:16 NIV

*W*e must trust as if it all depended on God and work as if it all depended on us.

CHARLES SPURGEON

I delight to do Your will, O my God.

PSALM 40:8 NKJV

*Yesterday is just experience, but tomorrow is glistening with purpose—
and today is the channel leading from one to the other.*

BARBARA JOHNSON

You have made known to me the ways of life:
You will make me full of joy in Your presence.

ACTS 2:28 NKJV

Far away, there in the sunshine, are my highest aspirations. I may not reach them but I can look up and see their beauty, believe in them, and try to follow where they lead.

LOUISA MAY ALCOTT

I will give you hidden treasures, riches stored in secret places,
so that you may know that I am the Lord.

ISAIAH 45:3 NIV

God shall be my hope, my stay, my guide and lantern to my feet.

I will turn darkness to light in front of them and rough places into level ground.

ISAIAH 42:16 HCSB

[*God*] wants to paint a beautiful portrait of His Son in and through your life.
A painting like no other in all of time.

Joni Eareckson Tada

For we are God's masterpiece. He has created us anew in Christ Jesus, so we can do the good things he planned for us long ago.

EPHESIANS 2:10 NLT

Every time Jesus sees that there is a possibility of giving us
more than we know how to ask for, He does so.

OLE HALLESBY

Now to Him who is able to do far more abundantly beyond all that we ask or think, according to the power that works within us, to Him be the glory.

EPHESIANS 3:20–21 NASB

In the process of creation and relationship, what seems mundane
and trivial may show itself to be holy, precious, part of a pattern.

LUCI SHAW

*T*ake your everyday, ordinary life—your sleeping, eating, going-to-work, and walking-around life—and place it before God as an offering. Embracing what God does for you is the best thing you can do for him.

ROMANS 12:1–2 MSG

God walks with us.... He scoops us up in His arms or simply sits with us in silent strength until we cannot avoid the awesome recognition that, yes, even now, He is here.

GLORIA GAITHER

He made the entire human race and made the earth hospitable, with plenty of time and space for living so we could seek after God, and not just grope around in the dark but actually find him.... He's not remote; he's near.

ACTS 17:26–27 MSG

He paints the lily of the field,
Perfumes each lily bell;
If He so loves the little flowers,
I know He loves me well.

MARIA STRAUS

For He will give His angels charge concerning you, to guard you in all your ways.

PSALM 91:11 NASB

We are made to reach out beyond our grasp.

OSWALD CHAMBERS

This command I am giving you today is not too difficult for you, and it is not beyond your reach.

DEUTERONOMY 30:11 NLT

Caring words, friendship, affectionate touch—all of these have a healing quality.
Why? Because we were all created by God to give and receive love.

JACK FROST

Go after a life of love as if your life depended on it—
because it does. Give yourselves to the gifts God gives you.

1 CORINTHIANS 14:1 MSG

It is necessary that we dream now and then. No one ever achieved anything from the smallest to the greatest unless the dream was dreamed first.

LAURA INGALLS WILDER

May he grant your heart's desires and make all your plans succeed.

PSALM 20:4 NLT

Lift up your eyes. Your heavenly Father waits to bless you—in inconceivable ways to make your life what you never dreamed it could be.

ANNE ORTLUND

....

....

....

....

....

....

....

....

....

....

....

....

....

....

....

I lift up my eyes to the mountains—
where does my help come from?
My help comes from the Lord,
the Maker of heaven and earth.

PSALM 121:1–2 NIV

It is only with the heart that one can see rightly. What is essential is invisible to the eye.

ANTOINE DE SAINT-EXUPÉRY

*M*an looks on the outward appearance, but the Lord looks on the heart.

1 Samuel 16:7 AMP

You have a unique message to deliver, a unique song to sing, a unique act of love to bestow. This message, this song, and this act of love have been entrusted exclusively to the one and only you.

JOHN POWELL, SJ

Isn't everything you have and everything you are sheer gifts from God?

1 Corinthians 4:7 MSG

*Begin today! No matter how feeble the light, let it shine as best it may.
The world may need just that quality of light which you have.*

HENRY C. BLINN

In the same way, let your light shine before others,
that they may see your good deeds and glorify your Father in heaven.

MATTHEW 5:16 NIV

*W*here are you? Start there. Openly and freely
declare your need to the One who cares deeply.

CHARLES R. SWINDOLL

He redeems your life from the Pit;
He crowns you with faithful love and compassion.

You pay God a compliment by asking great things of Him.

This is what I have asked of God for you:
that you will be encouraged and knit together by strong ties of love.

COLOSSIANS 2:2 TLB

In Love's service, only wounded soldiers can serve.

BRENNAN MANNING

My strength is made perfect in weakness.

2 CORINTHIANS 12:9 NKJV

*G*reat relief and satisfaction can come from seeking God's priorities for us in each season.

BETH MOORE

To everything there is a season, a time for every purpose under heaven.

ECCLESIASTES 3:1 NKJV

God gives everyone a special gift and a special place to use it.

Each of you should continue to live in whatever situation the Lord has placed you, and remain as you were when God first called you.

1 Corinthians 7:17 nlt

Before anything else, above all else, beyond everything else,
God loves us. God loves us extravagantly, ridiculously, without limit or condition.
God is in love with us...God yearns for us.

ROBERTA BONDI

The Lord *your God...will exult over you with joy,*
He will be quiet in His love, He will rejoice over you with shouts of joy.

ZEPHANIAH 3:17 NASB

*N*othing can separate you from His love, absolutely nothing....
God is enough for time, and God is enough for eternity. God is enough!

HANNAH WHITALL SMITH

I am convinced that nothing can ever separate us from God's love.
Neither death nor life, neither angels nor demons, neither our fears
for today nor our worries about tomorrow—not even the powers
of hell can separate us from God's love.

ROMANS 8:38 NLT

Take what was your past and light it as a bonfire to be a beacon for others.

LISA BEVERE

We are glad to seem weak if it helps show that you are actually strong.

2 CORINTHIANS 13:9 NLT

God has called us into the joyous ministry of giving His love away to others.

DON LESSIN

My [brimming] cup runs over.

PSALM 23:5 AMP

Your dreams grow holy put into action.

Let us not love with words or speech but with actions and in truth.

1 JOHN 3:18 NIV

Do not be afraid to enter the cloud that is settling down on your life. God is in it. The other side is radiant with His glory.

L. B. COWMAN

*I*n the fear of the Lord there is strong confidence,
and His children will have a place of refuge.

PROVERBS 14:26 NKJV

*N*othing that happens to me is meaningless, and that it is good for us
all that it should be so, even if it runs counter to our own wishes....
I'm here for some purpose, and I only hope I may fulfill it.

DIETRICH BONHOEFFER

God is able to make all grace abound to you, so that always having all sufficiency in everything, you may have an abundance for every good deed.

2 CORINTHIANS 9:8 NASB

*You and I are the creatures He prizes above the rest of His creation.
We are made in His image.*

JOHN FISHER

God created mankind in his own image.

GENESIS 1:27 NIV

*G*od has designs on our future...and He has designed us for the future.
He has given us something to do in the future that no one else can do.

It's in Christ that we find out who we are and what we are living for.
Long before we first heard of Christ and got our hopes up, he had his eye on us.

EPHESIANS 1:11 MSG

God's Word has the power to light our way and to clear the debris
that has covered the path so we can walk in it.

LISA BEVERE

....

....

....

....

....

....

....

....

....

....

....

....

....

....

....

....

....

....

....

The Lord God is my Strength, my personal bravery,
and my invincible army; He makes my feet like hinds' feet and will
make me to walk [not to stand still in terror, but to walk].

HABAKKUK 3:19 AMP

God wants to continually add to us, to develop and enlarge us—
always building on what He has already taught and built in us.

A. B. SIMPSON

*C*ome, let us go up to the mountain of the LORD....
There he will teach us his ways, and we will walk in his paths.

MICAH 4:2 NLT

*N*ever be afraid to trust an unknown future to a known God.

CORRIE TEN BOOM

*N*o eye has seen, no ear has heard, and no mind has imagined
what God has prepared for those who love him.

1 CORINTHIANS 2:9 NLT

The human contribution is the essential ingredient.
It is only in the giving of oneself to others that we truly live.

ETHEL PERCY ANDRUS

*D*ear friends, if God loved us in this way, we also must love one another.

1 JOHN 4:11 HCSB

*God created the universe, but He also created you. God knows you,
God loves you, and God cares about the tiniest details of your life.*

BRUCE BICKEL AND STAN JANTZ

You know when I sit down and when I rise up.... You scrutinize my path and my lying down, and are intimately acquainted with all my ways.

PSALM 139:2–3 NASB

God's plan will always be greater and more beautiful than all your disappointments.

*M*ay you have the power to understand, as all God's people should,
how wide, how long, how high, and how deep his love is.

EPHESIANS 3:18 NLT

Always be in a state of expectancy, and see that you
leave room for God to come in as He likes.

OSWALD CHAMBERS

He who did not spare His own Son, but delivered Him over for us all,
how will He not also with Him freely give us all things?

ROMANS 8:32 NASB

God waits for us in the inner sanctuary of the soul. He welcomes us there.

RICHARD J. FOSTER

The Lord [earnestly] waits [expecting, looking, and longing] to be gracious to you.

Isaiah 30:18 AMP

Go confidently in the direction of your dreams! Live the life you've imagined.

HENRY DAVID THOREAU

Do not be afraid, for I have ransomed you.
I have called you by name; you are mine.

ISAIAH 43:1 NLT

Live your life while you have it. Life is a splendid gift—there is nothing small about it.

FLORENCE NIGHTINGALE

To enjoy your work and accept your lot in life—this is indeed a gift from God.

ECCLESIASTES 5:19 NLT

How glorious the splendor of a human heart that trusts that it is loved!

BRENNAN MANNING

*"Though the mountains move and the hills shake,
My love will not be removed from you and My covenant of peace
will not be shaken," says your compassionate Lord.*

ISAIAH 54:10 HCSB

*G*od will never let you be shaken or moved from your place near His heart.

JONI EARECKSON TADA

*Like a shepherd He will tend His flock, in His arm He will gather
the lambs and carry them in His bosom.*

ISAIAH 40:11 NASB

Love is the seed of all hope. It is the enticement to trust, to risk, to try, and to go on.

GLORIA GAITHER

[*Love*] bears all things, believes all things, hopes all things,
endures all things.

1 CORINTHIANS 13:7 NKJV

God surpasses our dreams when we reach past our personal plans and agenda to grab
the hand of Christ and walk the path He chose for us. He is obligated to keep
us dissatisfied until we come to Him and His plan for complete satisfaction.

BETH MOORE

I shall be fully satisfied, when I awake [to find myself] beholding Your form
[and having sweet communion with You].

PSALM 17:15 AMP

When I need a dose of wonder I wait for a clear night and go look for the stars.
MADELEINE L'ENGLE

When I look at the night sky and see the work of your fingers—
the moon and the stars you set in place—
what are mere mortals that you should think about them,
human beings that you should care for them?

PSALM 8:3–4 NLT

God created us with an overwhelming desire to soar.... He designed us to be
tremendously productive and to "mount up with wings like eagles,"
realistically dreaming of what He can do with our potential.

CAROL KENT

We are praying, too, that you will be filled with his mighty, glorious strength so that you can keep going no matter what happens—always full of the joy of the Lord.

COLOSSIANS 1:11 TLB

*Some days, it is enough encouragement just to watch the clouds break up
and disappear, leaving behind a blue patch of sky and bright sunshine
that is so warm upon my face. It's a glimpse of divinity; a kiss from heaven.*

*The path of the righteous is like the light of dawn,
that shines brighter and brighter until the full day.*

PROVERBS 4:18 NASB

Thanksgiving—always precedes the miracle.

ANN VOSKAMP

The LORD's lovingkindnesses indeed never cease, for His compassions never fail.
They are new every morning; great is Your faithfulness.

LAMENTATIONS 3:21–23 NASB

*N*ever yield to gloomy anticipation. Place your hope and confidence in God. He has no record of failure.

MRS. CHARLES E COWMAN

Surely goodness and mercy shall follow me all the days of my life;
and I will dwell in the house of the Lord forever.

PSALM 23:6 NKJV

*It is difficult to say what is impossible, for the dream of yesterday
is the hope of today and the reality of tomorrow.*

ROBERT H. GODDARD

Now faith is the substance of things hoped for, the evidence of things not seen.

HEBREWS 11:1 NKJV

Real joy comes not from ease or riches or from the praise of men,
but from doing something worthwhile.

Joyful are people of integrity, who follow the instructions of the Lord. Joyful are those who obey his laws and search for him with all their hearts.

PSALM 119:1–2 NLT

There is no greater joy nor greater reward than to make
a fundamental difference in someone's life.

MARY ROSE MCGEADY

You shall love your neighbor as yourself.

GALATIANS 5:14 NASB

You are stronger than you thought. Stretch out your arms like mighty branches even if, for now, they're as thin as sticks. It is to your Father's glory that you bear much fruit.

BETH MOORE

*B*lessed is the one who trusts in the Lord, whose confidence is in him.
They will be like a tree planted by the water that sends out its roots by the stream.

Jeremiah 17:7–8 niv

We have been in God's thought from all eternity,
and in His creative love, His attention never leaves us.

Michael Quoist

How ow precious also are Your thoughts to me, O God! How vast is the sum of them! If I should count them, they would outnumber the sand.

PSALM 139:17–18 NASB

We are all cups, constantly and quietly being filled. The trick is, knowing how to tip ourselves over and let the beautiful stuff out.

RAY BRADBURY

*M*ay the God of hope fill you with all joy and peace as you trust in him,
so that you may overflow with hope.

ROMANS 15:13 NIV

Take courage. We walk in the wilderness today but in the Promised Land tomorrow.

D. L. MOODY

Give all your worries and cares to God, for he cares about you.

1 PETER 5:7 NLT

*O*pen your hearts to the love God instills.... God loves you tenderly.
What He gives you is not to be kept under lock and key, but to be shared.

*F*or God has not given us a spirit of fearfulness,
but one of power, love, and sound judgment.

2 Timothy 1:7 HCSB

God's fingers can touch nothing but to mold it into loveliness.

GEORGE MACDONALD

God has made everything beautiful for its own time.

ECCLESIASTES 3:11 NLT

*G*od has a wonderful plan for each person He has chosen. He knew even before
He created this world what beauty He would bring forth from our lives.

LOUIS B. WYLY

*Y*ou will be given a new name by the Lᴏʀᴅ's own mouth. The Lᴏʀᴅ will hold you in his hand for all to see—a splendid crown in the hand of God.

Isᴀɪᴀʜ 62:2–3 ɴʟᴛ

*G*od gives us all gifts, special abilities that we are entrusted
with developing to help serve Him and serve others.

I pray that the eyes of your heart may be enlightened
in order that you may know the hope to which he has called you.

EPHESIANS 1:18 NIV

Ellie Claire® Gift & Paper Expressions
Franklin, TN 37067
EllieClaire.com
Ellie Claire is a registered trademark of Worthy Media, Inc.

God Has a Design for Your Life Journal
© 2015 by Ellie Claire
Published by Ellie Claire, an imprint of Worthy Publishing Group, a division of Worthy Media, Inc.

ISBN 978-1-63326-057-3

Stock or custom editions of Ellie Claire titles may be purchased in bulk for educational, business, ministry, fund-raising, or sales promotional use. For information, please e-mail info@EllieClaire.com.

Compiled by Jill Olson
Images from Shutterstock.com
Cover and interior design by Melissa Reagan

Printed in China

2 3 4 5 6 7 8 9 10 – 20 19 18 17 16 15